Dear Sis A Place for Your Heart

A Reflection and Prayer Journal

Dr. Tache' Vereen

Dear Sis: A Place for Your Heart: A Reflection & Prayer Journal

Book Cover & Layout Design: Abu Bakar Javed

Published by: DOC with TV LLC

Printed in the United States of America

www.docwithtv.com

ISBN: 979-8-9993418-2-2

Sis, this is your space. A place for your heart to breathe, reflect, and be refreshed. Let these pages be a sacred conversation between you and God. Write freely. Pray boldly. Dream again. You are seen, loved, and never alone.

— Dr. Tache' Vereen

Dear God,

My Heart Today ...

Quiet Reflections...

Prayer Notes . . .

Pour it out, Sis...

Dear God,

My Heart Today ...

Quiet Reflections...

Prayer Notes . . .

Pour it out, Sis...

Dear God,

My Heart Today ...

Quiet Reflections...

Prayer Notes . . .

Pour it out, Sis...

Dear God,

My Heart Today ...

Quiet Reflections...

Prayer Notes ...

Pour it out, Sis...

Dear God,

My Heart Today ...

Quiet Reflections...

Prayer Notes . . .

Pour it out, Sis...

Dear God,

My Heart Today ...

Quiet Reflections...

Prayer Notes . . .

Pour it out, Sis...

Dear God,

My Heart Today ...

Quiet Reflections...

Prayer Notes . . .

Pour it out, Sis...

Dear God,

My Heart Today ...

Quiet Reflections...

Prayer Notes . . .

Pour it out, Sis...

Dear God,

My Heart Today ...

Quiet Reflections...

Prayer Notes . . .

Pour it out, Sis...

Dear God,

My Heart Today ...

Quiet Reflections...

Prayer Notes ...

Pour it out, Sis . . .

Dear God,

My Heart Today ...

Quiet Reflections...

Prayer Notes . . .

Pour it out, Sis...

Dear God,

My Heart Today ...

Quiet Reflections...

Prayer Notes . . .

Pour it out, Sis...

Dear God,

My Heart Today ...

Quiet Reflections...

Prayer Notes . . .

Pour it out, Sis...

Dear God,

My Heart Today ...

Quiet Reflections...

Prayer Notes ...

Pour it out, Sis...

Dear God,

My Heart Today ...

Quiet Reflections...

Prayer Notes . . .

Pour it out, Sis…

Dear God,

My Heart Today ...

Quiet Reflections...

Prayer Notes . . .

Pour it out, Sis…

Dear God,

My Heart Today ...

Quiet Reflections...

Prayer Notes . . .

Pour it out, Sis...

Dear God,

My Heart Today ...

Quiet Reflections...

Prayer Notes …

Pour it out, Sis . . .

Dear God,

My Heart Today ...

Quiet Reflections...

Prayer Notes . . .

Pour it out, Sis...

Dear God,

My Heart Today ...

Quiet Reflections...

Prayer Notes ...

Pour it out, Sis...

Dear God,

My Heart Today ...

Quiet Reflections...

Prayer Notes . . .

Pour it out, Sis...

Dear God,

My Heart Today ...

Quiet Reflections...

Prayer Notes ...

Pour it out, Sis...

Dear God,

My Heart Today ...

Quiet Reflections...

Prayer Notes . . .

Pour it out, Sis…

Dear God,

My Heart Today ...

Quiet Reflections...

Prayer Notes . . .

Pour it out, Sis...

Dear God,

My Heart Today ...

Quiet Reflections...

Prayer Notes ...

Pour it out, Sis...

Dear God,

My Heart Today ...

Quiet Reflections...

Prayer Notes . . .

Pour it out, Sis…

Dear God,

My Heart Today ...

Quiet Reflections...

Prayer Notes . . .

Pour it out, Sis...

Dear God,

My Heart Today ...

Quiet Reflections...

Prayer Notes ...

Pour it out, Sis . . .

Dear God,

My Heart Today ...

Quiet Reflections...

Prayer Notes . . .

Pour it out, Sis…

Dear God,

My Heart Today ...

Quiet Reflections...

Prayer Notes . . .

Pour it out, Sis...

Sis, you've poured your heart out — now let God fill it up. Keep writing. Keep believing. Keep growing. You are loved more than you know.

— Dr. Tache' Vereen

www.ingramcontent.com/pod-product-compliance
Lightning Source LLC
Chambersburg PA
CBHW031303120626
46545CB00007B/2964
* 9 7 9 8 9 9 9 3 4 1 8 2 2 *